NEW EDITION

THE COLONIES
OF STOCKBRIDGE

Rosemary J Pipes

Lomond Books

Acknowledgements

Thanks are due to: Edinburgh City Libraries (Figures 1, 5, 7, 8, 10, 11, 13, 14, 18, cover); Richard Roger (map 2); National Galleries of Scotland, Edinburgh (Figures 3 and 4); National Museums of Scotland (21); Michael Wolchover and Doug Clapperton for taking some of the photographs; David Hogg for the drawings on pages 25, 30 and 56.

The quotations on pages 20 and 46 are from *James Duff Brown – Portrait of a Library Pioneer* by Dr W. A. Munford (The Library Association, 1968).

The photo on the back cover shows the original Falshaw Bridge, built in 1876 and opened by Lord Provost James Falshaw in May 1877.

ISBN 0947782-222
First edition: 1984
Second edition: 1998

Published by Lomond Books, Edinburgh
Cover design and layout by The Graphics Company, Edinburgh
Printed by Bell & Bain, Glasgow
Typeset in Galliard 10½ on 13½ point

Contents

Preface
to the new edition

Following the publication of the first edition of this book in 1984, feedback from readers and further research have pointed to some significant omissions in the original text. First, it was felt that the book did not contain enough material relating to the social history of the Stockbridge Colonies, in particular the recent history as recalled by people still living in the area. In response to this concern, a Colonies oral history group was formed in the early 1990s and interviews were conducted with over 20 local residents who had lived in the Colonies for most or all or their lives and whose memories of the area went back 60 years or more. Given the quantity and nature of the material collected by the group, it was clear that to do it justice a separate publication was needed rather than an expanded version of this book. Thus, in 1993, a collection of extracts from the interviews was published in a new book called *No Whistling on a Sunday*, thereby adding a much needed personal dimension to the history of the houses.

Another omission from the first edition was a description of how the Colonies came to get their name, and what that name means. This omission been put right by the addition of a new sub-section in the second chapter (see pages 34-35).

At the time when the original book was written, the Edinburgh Cooperative Building Company Minute books for the years 1861-1865 and 1875-1883 were missing from the collection in East Register House. Unfortunately these are still missing, but what has appeared since that time is a collection of personal papers belonging to Daniel William Kemp, one-time Director of the Cooperative, and the son of Daniel Kemp, one of the first Directors, after whom Kemp Place is named. Some of the material contained in these papers has been included in this second edition, as have some photographs that came to light during recent research.

September 1998

Introduction

Over a century ago, the writer and journalist Hugh Gilzean Reid wrote and published the following *Story of John Wilson*. The purpose of Reid's story was to offer 'instruction and hope to all workers and the many who seek to help in providing homes for the people'.

Although romantic and moralistic in tone, and sometimes fanciful in detail, the story conveys something of the flavour of the times, and serves again here as an introduction both to the Colonies of Stockbridge and to one of the most remarkable cooperative housing ventures in Edinburgh's history.

'One evening towards the close of 1861, John Wilson and Mary Brown might have been seen walking, arm-in-arm, down by Glenogle Park – now a very pleasant part of the outskirts of Edinburgh. The Cooperative Company had purchased a piece of land there, and commenced building on it.

"I have resolved" said John quietly, "never to take you to any of those dingy hovels off the High Street, or even to those barrack-like blocks, although we should wait ever so long."

"You are right," was the ready response. "How horrible it must be to live in those dark closes, and be forced to associate, even in any degree, with the people one sees there! How sorry I often am for poor Mrs. Smith. I called up on her yesterday, and she had just been papering her little dingy rooms with a red and white paper, but, as she truly said, it was of little use – the rain would soon be down on the walls again. And then, such language as we heard among some drunken neighbours, who had just come into the other half of the of the house! It was sad to see the children clinging to their mother through terror of them and to think of the influence the example might have. I felt as if I had escaped from a den of lions when I once got out into the clear light of heaven."

"Yes Mary; I am glad that you understand it all so well: that is the fate of most of us working men when we get married, and even sometimes while we live in lodgings. But I have been determined, with God's help, to commence life with you in other and better circumstances; and at last the possibility is placed within our reach. I have taken twenty shares in the Cooperative Building Company, and you will help me to pay them up as speedily as possible. We could do so at the rate of one shilling a week, but the sooner the money is deposited the better, as we shall have the more profit, and I have strong confidence in the movement. The houses will be ready in a few weeks, and I mean to purchase one."

"To buy a house, John! – you must be dreaming."

"It seems like a dream," observed John; "but it is as much a reality as our wedding, and I will tell you how. There is the very house I've fixed upon, No. – Reid Terrace; it has three neat airy rooms and a closet; and see – twenty square yards for a garden in front, and a fine large green behind for drying the clothes. It has all conveniences, too. I know it is substantially built; and then, the pleasant situation – the trees behind there, and a street when the other row of houses comes to be built, of more than sixty feet wide!"

"It is grand this!" exclaimed Mary, as she entered. "An entrance-door all to ourselves; those common stairs are always dirty; and where so many are care-less, there is no heart in trying to keep them clean. But what about the buying?"

John brightened up as he proceeded. "It's all through this cooperative principle. I will pay up my shares as soon as we can; and as I am a good workman, the Company gives me the best wages going. Well, we have as much money, you know, as will furnish the house comfortably, and pay all preliminary expenses."

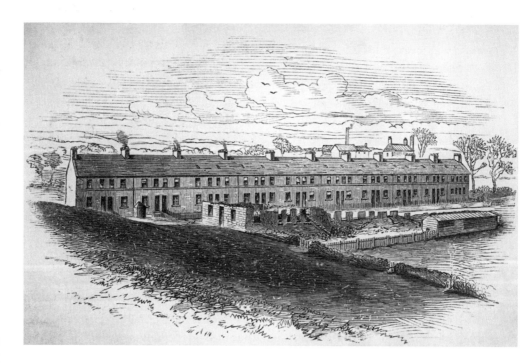

1 A Victorian etching showing Reid Terrace and the beginnings of Hugh Miller Place, viewed from the south east.

"But," interrupted Mary, "where is the money to buy the house?"

"Wait a little," said John, with characteristic calmness; "it needs time to explain this wonderful scheme. The cost of the house is £130, and I calculate we shall have at least £5 over the marriage and furnishings. Well, in accordance with an arrangement between our Society and it, the Property Investment Company will advance the balance of £125 on the security of the title-deeds. Then we will pay them £13 a year for fourteen years, when the house will become really and truly our own. Now Robert Smith is paying at the rate of £11 for that abominable place of his, and is no better at the year's end than he was at the beginning, but a great deal worse; so, you see, for that £2 a year, or £28 altogether, we shall actually buy this fine house; and, while the process is going on, we shall have a comfortable home – all our own. And more, if the Company prospers – and as we shall all be working for ourselves, and directly interested in doing the most and the best, there is every prospect of success – the yearly profit on my shares will make up the difference between the amount we shall have to pay and ordinary rent for a very moderate house; so that we have a house of our own for next to nothing. The savings bank does not allow much; and where can we find any other safe investment?"

Mary opened her eyes, and grasping by faith in John what sight could not fully compass, she clapped her hands with joy.

John Wilson and Mary Brown were married in December 1862, and long ago they actually owned the house which cost them nothing save forethought, economy, and perseverance; and they are gradually becoming the possessors of other houses for their children by the same simple process.

"I am sorry, very sorry for poor Mrs. Smith," wailed Mary across the comfortably-stored table, at which sat her husband and three blooming children. "Robert wouldn't join the Company, and he would go to the public house; and there he is now, getting old, and everything going to wreck. We cannot be too thankful that we were enabled to forsake the one and hold by the other. I did not clearly see it all that day you first opened it up to me; but I feel it all now."

John Wilson, a real personality ever teaching and preaching the new gospel of self-help, is only a type of the sober and industrious workmen who have, through this cooperative agency, been comfortably housed, and who have become the proud and privileged owners of their beautiful dwellings. To all workers and to many who seek to help in providing homes for the people, the story is full of instruction and hope.'

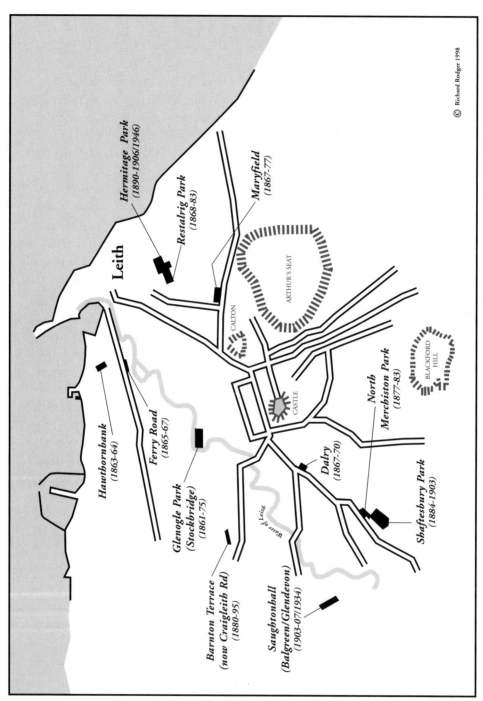

© Richard Rodger 1998

Leith

Hermitage Park
(1890-1906/1946)

Restalrig Park
(1868-83)

Maryfield
(1867-77)

ARTHUR'S SEAT

CALTON

Hawthornbank
(1863-64)

Ferry Road
(1865-67)

Glenogle Park
(Stockbridge)
(1861-75)

CASTLE

Water of Leith

BLACKFORD
HILL

North
Merchiston Park
(1877-83)

Dalry
(1867-70)

Shaftesbury Park
(1884-1903)

Barnton Terrace
(now Craigleith Rd)
(1880-95)

Saughtonhall
(Balgreen/Glendevon)
(1903-07/1934)

2 The location of the housing developments built by the Edinburgh Cooperative Building Company.

The Edinburgh Cooperative Building Company Limited

The Cooperative Company described by Reid in his story was The Edinburgh Cooperative Building Company. Although best known for its nineteenth century 'colonies' of artisans' housing, it did in fact continue to build well into the twentieth century and only ceased to exist as a cooperative in 1945 when it became an ordinary building contractor – Edinburgh Building Contractors Ltd.

By far the most interesting period in the life of the Company, and the period of most relevance to this history, was the first ten to fifteen years, from 1861 to the mid 1870s. It was the achievement of those early years that later earned the Company its reputation as 'the most important and enduring experiment in cooperative house building in Edinburgh.' By the end of that period, it had built on at least five sites around the city (see map 2) and had completed over one thousand separate dwellings.

As the first of the sites to be developed by the Cooperative, the one at Glenogle Road has a very special place in its history. This 'colony', more than any of the others, provides the most apt monument both to the Cooperative and to many of those who inspired and worked for it. It is their names that were chosen for the first terraces, and it is the symbols of the many trades involved that appear on the sculpted gable-end plaques.

BEGINNINGS

From amongst the seven men's names that were chosen for the terraces, three in particular take the story of the Cooperative back to its beginnings in mid-Victorian Edinburgh. These are Hugh Miller (1802-1856), stonemason, writer, journalist and celebrated geologist; Hugh Gilzean Reid (1836-1911), journalist and later Liberal MP; and James Colville (1822-1892), stonemason and the first Manager of the Cooperative. Add to these a fourth – The Reverend Doctor James Begg (1808-1883) – and the list of 'founders' is virtually complete.

3 Hugh Miller, posing for the camera of David Octavius Hill in the Calton cemetery, 1843. Miller used this picture of himself dressed in his stonemason's attire to illustrate an article he wrote for *The Witness* newspaper. The caption he gave the picture was: 'A bonneted mechanic rests over his mallet on a tombstone – his one arm bared above his elbow; the other wrapped in the well-established shirt folds and resting on a grotesque sculpture.'

4 The Reverend James Begg (left), Hugh Miller (centre) and Dr Thomas Guthrie in conspiratorial mood. The three men were collaborators in the Disruption of 1843 when Begg, Guthrie and many other Scottish clergy walked out of the Church Assembly to form their own Free Church.

Of the four men, Hugh Miller's link with the Cooperative was the most remote. He probably never met either Reid or Colville, but James Begg was a close acquaintance. The reason for their meeting, and a great bond between them, was the recently formed Free Church. Begg was one of its first ministers and Miller edited its newspaper, *The Witness.* Another link between them was their shared concern for the social, economic, physical and moral welfare of Edinburgh's rapidly growing working population. Both men held the view that poverty, depravity and ill-health were inextricably linked with insanitary, overcrowded and overpriced tenement living, and they believed that the first step towards the 'improvement' of the working classes was to improve their dwellings. As Miller once wrote – 'It is idle to speak of reform, and almost idle to speak of moral reform, when we contemplate the dwellings of a large portion of the working population.... We must devise some plan by which proper

5 Sir Hugh Gilzean Reid

buildings shall be erected, and insure the future well-being of the people....'
Had Hugh Miller lived only five more years, he would have seen just such a
plan turned into reality by men of his own trade. As it was, the pioneering
work was left to James Begg, and later to Hugh Gilzean Reid, another ardent
Free Church supporter, a journalist and a champion of the working classes.

Reid arrived in Edinburgh in the late 1850s to become editor of the *Edinburgh Weekly News*. He, like Begg, had a keen interest in the idea of worker
cooperation, and in 1860, at the age of twenty-four, he became secretary of
the 'nine hours movement' in Edinburgh. This nation-wide movement for the

reduction of the working day from ten to nine hours was generally regarded as 'a great and important means of improving the physical, moral, social and intellectual condition of the working classes'. In Edinburgh it was supported by most trades, but it was the stonemasons and joiners who made the first moves to seek the nine-hour day. They wrote to their employers requesting reduced hours in exchange for a reduction in wages, but were refused. As a result, 865 masons and 400 joiners were 'locked out' from February to May 1861. It was during this period of forced unemployment that some of the masons decided to think seriously about forming their own cooperative company, with the aim of building houses for themselves and other artisans to buy and to live in.

When writing in later years, Hugh Gilzean Reid recalls how the masons made frequent visits to his High Street office to discuss their scheme. Of those involved in these early discussions, he mentions only one by name – James Colville. By then in his early 40s, Colville had already been actively involved in union affairs and had served his time as President of the Masons' Union. Very little is known about his early life so it is only possible to guess at the reasons for his involvement with Reid and Begg. It may have been a Free Church connection, or simply a shared interest in the cooperative ideal. In any event, his qualities as a 'stalwart workman' were obviously recognised by Begg and Reid, and by his fellow masons who elected him first Manager of the Cooperative – a position he continued to hold until 1889 when he finally retired, aged 67.

AIMS AND METHODS

The decision to form a cooperative building company was finally taken by a meeting of stonemasons in April 1861. A month later, on May 25, The Edinburgh Cooperative Building Company Limited officially started business. According to its Articles of Association, the business was fairly broadly defined as 'the carrying on of building in all its branches, including joiner work as well as mason work, and every other work incidental or conducive to the business of building in all its branches, and that either by contract or speculation; including the acquisition, either by purchase, lease or other tenure, of house property and of land, for the purpose of erecting thereon houses and other buildings.'

Such a description could easily apply to any commercial building business, but in the case of the Cooperative, it was the underlying aim that set it apart from other contemporary enterprises. In the words of an observer at the time when building began at Stockbridge, this aim was 'to build and sell the houses, and with the money thus received, not only to pay interest on the capital, but to build and sell again, until the supply of workmen's houses shall meet the demand...Everything, however, depends on the energy of the men themselves.'

To finance its operations, the Cooperative needed capital and this was acquired through the sale of shares. It was possible to become a partner in the Cooperative by buying one or more one pound shares either by down payment or in five-shilling instalments to be paid over a year. Shares earned their holders a related number of votes at General Meetings, plus a portion of Company profits which were distributed annually in the form of a dividend. The management of Company affairs was conducted by an elected Committee of Management comprising no more than twenty Directors of whom ten had to be building operatives, including the Chairman, one of the two Vice-Presidents, and the Manager. The only paid officials were the Manager, Secretary and Treasurer.

Apart from the condition that ten Directors should be building operatives, membership of the Cooperative was open to anyone, just as anyone was eligible to buy or live in the houses it built. In practice, however, it was to skilled artisans that the Cooperative had most appeal and it was they who made up the vast majority of its shareholders and house buyers in the early years. For example, of the 341 shareholders registered by June 1862, 132 were stonemasons, and the rest represented over sixty other trades including joinery, brassfounding, glasscutting, printing and decorating. Only a handful of these initial subscribers came from the professions and from better paid clerical occupations, but even fewer were unskilled labourers.

Even amongst the artisan class, however, the level of income was such that very few people could afford to buy a house outright. Indeed, some would have had difficulty in raising the £1 needed to buy a share in the Company. How, then, were potential buyers to find the money to buy a house costing over £100? The solution was found through the cooperation of certain Property Investment Companies in the city who were prepared to lend Cooperative house buyers over £100 on security of the title deeds. Through this arrangement it was possible for anyone on a modest but secure income to take immediate possession of one of the Company's houses by paying a deposit of £5. If the house cost £130 to buy, the remaining £125 was borrowed from the Property Investment Company and the loan plus interest paid back over a period of up to fourteen years. For those house buyers who were also shareholders, there was the added bonus of the annual dividend which could go some way towards financing the loan repayments and other costs, such as the feu duty, rates and general maintenance and repairs of the building.

This system of loan and purchase continued until 1870 when the Cooperative started its own scheme whereby house buyers paid a deposit then paid off the cost of the house in monthly or half-yearly instalments over fourteen or,

6 These villas at Barnton Terrace (now part of Craigleith Road) were built by the Cooperative in 1877 and were among the grandest and most expensive houses it ever constructed. There were nine in the row, and selling prices ranged from £600 to £1000 per house.

later, twenty-one years. Such a system of payment was made possible because in 1867 the Company started its own deposit scheme for shareholders and others. The reservoir of money created by this scheme was used to finance new building as well as to support the instalment scheme, and it had the advantage of providing the depositors with extra unearned income in the form of interest on their deposits.

Given the number of years over which the Edinburgh Cooperative Building Company continued to build, it isn't surprising that its character and fortunes showed some striking variations with time. The success of the early years was not sustained, and the Company eventually transformed into an ordinary trading concern, more interested in pleasing its shareholders than in pursuing reformist ideals. Nevertheless, as Hugh Gilzean Reid put it when writing about the Company in 1890, 'none the less real or necessary were the original motives, and none the less tangible and enduring are the results'.

The Colonies
of Stockbridge

THE SITE

Tucked into a sharp bend of the Water of Leith and flanked by steep banks to the north and south, the ground where the Colonies now stand presented an ideal site for the first of the Edinburgh Cooperative's projects. At the time when the Company began to build (1861), the site was far more rural and isolated than it is today. Cows grazed on the grassland which covered most of the flat valley floor, and a cluster of stone byres and cottages stood in the

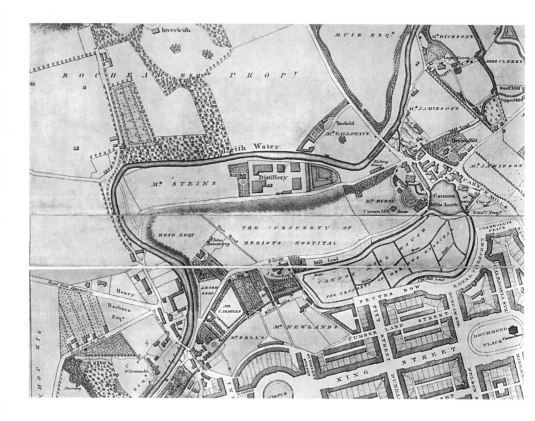

7 Part of Ainslie's map of Edinburgh, 1804

centre with a large and grander house to the east, set in its own grounds. Between the two there appears to have been a planned formal garden which was first laid out sometime between 1804 and 1817 (see maps 7 and 8) . The maps tell nothing about how this area was used, but given its position it could have been either a decorative landscaped garden, a more functional vegetable patch, or even a tree-edged paddock.

Access to the site was safest and easiest from the Canonmills end, along Water Lane (as Glenogle Road was then called). Anyone approaching from Stockbridge would have had to ford the river since the first footbridge was not built until 1865 (see page 20). The other routes into the area for pedestrians were Gabriel's Road to the south, and the path and stepping stones over the river to the north (see map 10).

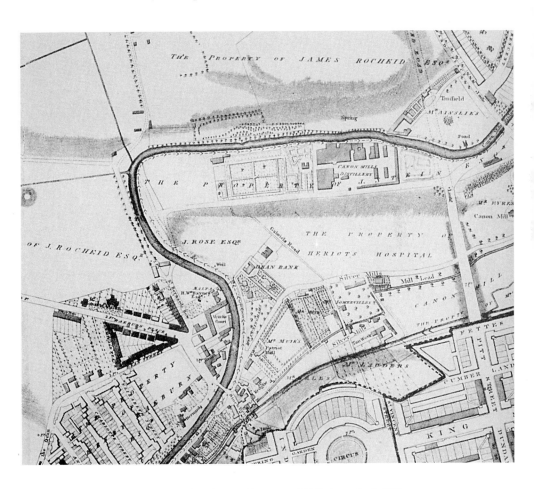

8 Part of Kirkwood's map of Edinburgh, 1817

When the Cooperative Directors signed the first feu contract for an acre of the site, it was owned by the heirs of James Haig, founder of the famous Haig whisky empire. Haig had chosen the east end of the site for his first distillery in Edinburgh and he and his relatives, the Steins, began building in the late 1770s. Ownership of the land and the distillery appears to have alternated between the two families over the years, and it seems likely that one or other of them built the large house just west of the distillery wall. Now part of Glenogle House, this building is shown as Canonmills Cottage on the 1853 map, but named Keif House in Post Office Directories and other written records. It may be that this house was originally built by the Haigs or Steins as a family home, but by the 1860s it was let to John Nicol, manager of a Chemists named Scott and Orr at 21 Dundas Street. The remaining ground and buildings were also let out to a tenant – Mr Thomas Haddow – a dairyman or 'cowfeeder.' Haddow probably managed the cattle and grassland, and also appears to have owned or run two dairies in Stockbridge.

9 The Glenogle Road maltings (previously Haig's whisky distillery) as they were in the early 1970s, just before demolition.

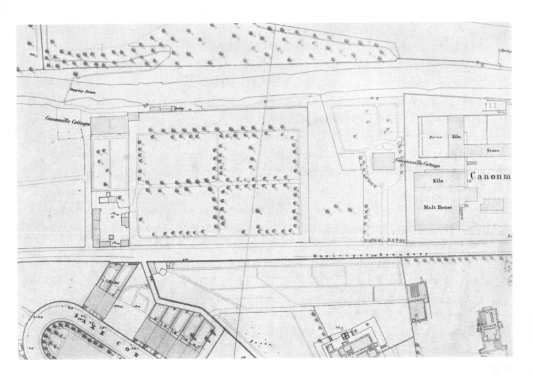

10 An extract from the 1853 OS map, showing Canonmills Cottage (now part of Glenogle House) and Canonmills Cottages and grounds.

As a site for artisan housing, the one at Water Lane had both attractions and drawbacks. Amongst its attractions were the flat ground for building and the relatively healthy, rural setting, only minutes away from the thriving industrial communities of Stockbridge and Canonmills, which could provide employment as well as shops and other services for the residents of the new 'colony'. A drawback of the site, which is now one of its main attractions, was the river itself. For nearly all of its length, the Water of Leith served as a source of power for hundreds of mills, and as a repository for the city's sewage and industrial waste. In 1866, the river was the subject of a lecture given at the Surgeons' Hall by Dr S. Macadam, who described it as 'a foul polluted stream, conveying faecal matter of the most disgusting and abominable kind, and evoking fetid emanations into the surrounding atmosphere'. Dr Macadam went on to describe how, during times of low rainfall, the mill lades drew off so much of the water that the river was reduced to a mere trickle and so left the stinking mud bed exposed to the open air.

For the early Colonies residents, dry summers must have been times to dread, but even worse were the wet winters when the river frequently rose to such heights that both lives and property could be lost. One of those early residents, James Duff Brown, spent his childhood at 3 Reid Terrace and at 19 Rintoul Place, and the notes he left of those early years of the 1860s include a vivid description of the floods – and worse.

'Where the Water of Leith crossed the roadway at the bottom of St Bernard's Row it was spanned by a wooden footbridge, and all wheeled traffic had to ford the stream. When the water was in flood it was quite common for horses and carts to be carried down the stream, either against the supports of the bridge, or beyond it, and there the horses were often attacked by horse leeches which abounded. Further down the river, or "doon the dam" as we called it, water rats were plentiful, and they continued right down to a place known locally as "Puddocky" and on past Warriston cemetery to Bonnington. The Water of Leith at that time ran between wooded banks,

11 A Victorian etching of the first wooden footbridge at Bridge Place, erected in 1865 and replaced in 1876 by a road bridge.

and there was a very pretty stretch between the bottom of Rintoul Place and Canonmills Bridge, where all was quiet and aquatic and bird life were much in evidence. The water was contaminated from the mills at the Dean Village and Stockbridge, and in later years various paper and dye works at Murrayfield added their drainings.'

Flooding on a more devastating scale is also described by Cumberland Hill in his history of Stockbridge (published in 1877). The first and most destructive flood he mentions was one that happened in 1659, causing 16 mills to be destroyed along the length of the river. The last to be mentioned by Hill was in 1879 when the water overflowed the newly erected Falshaw Bridge – an event which nearly happened again as recently as 1980. Other written records describe flood water filling basements in Warriston Crescent, and in the 1940s, Colonies houses in Bell Place suffered flood damage.

ACQUIRING THE SITE

The total area of the Water Lane site was over eight acres, and it would have been impossible for the Cooperative to feu it all in one Lot. Instead, it was agreed between the two parties – the Haig family and the Cooperative – that the site should be divided into a number of smaller Lots which could be negotiated separately over a period of time.

Lot one, which measured nearly two acres in area, was the first to be disponed and became the site of forty dwellings (Reid Terrace), a large drying green and a joiners' shop and Company site office (built where Bridge Place now stands). The annual feu duty was £20 per acre and the feu contract stated that the buildings were to be 'substantially built with stone and lime and roofed with slate and exclusive of chimney tops not to exceed forty-six feet'. This was only one of many conditions specified in the first and later feu contracts. Another was that 'it shall be unlawful to convert or permit to be converted any of the dwelling houses... into shebeens or brothels.' It was also unlawful to have any 'cow house, pig house or manufactury' on the ground.

Despite the fact that the Haigs' agent, Mr Stein, 'was very favourable to the general object' of the Cooperative, there must have been some legal difficulties or disagreements between the parties, because it was not until September 1862 that the first feu contract was finally signed – nearly one year after building had begun at Reid Terrace. From then on, however, progress went more smoothly and a second contract for Lots 2 and 3 was signed in April 1863 followed by another for Lots 4 and 5 two years later. This left nearly five acres of the site, between the distillery wall and Collins Place, still to be negotiated.

In the absence of the original feuing plans, it is not clear if this remaining area was subdivided into several Lots, or if it was marked off as one large Lot. In any event, it was finally agreed in January 1867 that the whole area should be feud as one Lot at a much increased annual feu of £36 per acre.

STAGES IN DEVELOPMENT

There are two plaques in the Colonies, one on the gable end of Collins Place and one on the wall of 17 Dunrobin Place, which mark two occasions in the development of the Colonies – the beginning in 1861 and the completion in 1911.

1861 was the year of formation of the Edinburgh Cooperative Building Company and Reid Terrace was the very first row of houses to be built. The foundation stone was laid at 4 o'clock on October 24 by The Reverend James

12 Commemorative plaques on the gable end of Collins Place (left) and the wall of 17 Dunrobin Place.

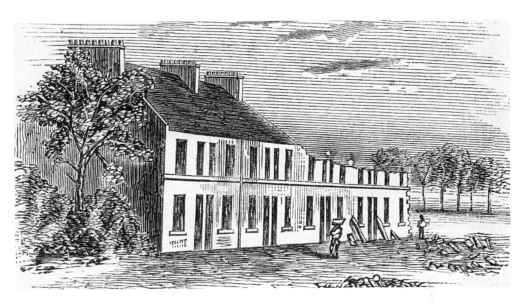

13 An early etching showing Reid Terrace under construction.

Begg whose opening words to the assembled crowd were: 'that what has now taken place will be in after ages recorded as a turning point in the history of Edinburgh.' He later insisted that 'the people who inhabit the houses will be as comfortable as those who dwell in Saxe-Coburg Place for they will look on the same trees and enjoy the benefits of the same river, such as it is'.

As the first terrace of houses to be built by the Company, Reid Terrace naturally became a show-piece for this new venture into cooperative house building. Would it prove to be popular? Would more shareholders be encouraged to put their money into the Company? The answer to both questions was obviously Yes. The houses in Reid Terrace were soon sold and the Company earned enough money from the sales and from shares to finance another two terraces (Hugh Miller and Rintoul) on Lots 2 and 3 of the ground. As with Reid Terrace, building began at the southern end and space for a communal drying and bleaching green was provided next to the river at the northern end.

The Cooperative managed to build at the rate of roughly one terrace per year, so by 1865 the first three were more or less completed. Another two, Colville and Collins, were begun as soon as the feu contract for Lots 3 and 4 was agreed, and these were finished by 1866-67. It was then that the Cooperative acquired the remaining four or five acres of the site. The west end was already occupied by Canonmills Cottages and other buildings and Keif House and gardens stood at the east. So where was building to begin? It was decided to start another terrace parallel to the rest, but at the east end of the ground.

The result was Bell Place which was completed within a year. At the same time, James Colville approached John Nicol, tenant of Keif House, to discuss the possibility of using the front and back gardens of the house as sites for two short terraces, to be built parallel to the main road (Water Lane). The front terrace was started first (Glenogle Place) followed by Glenogle Terrace, then Kemp Place was started a year later.

Meanwhile, plans had been laid for a new builders' yard, office and workshops in the middle of the newly acquired ground. By 1868 a smithy and stable for the horses had been built, plus an eighty-foot long joiners' shed which housed a newly purchased, steam-driven saw bench – the first to be bought by the Cooperative. Canonmills Cottages were incorporated into this new complex of buildings which grew and changed over the years until it was finally demolished towards the end of the nineteenth century.

Following completion of Kemp Place in 1869, building started at Avondale Place which was the last complete terrace to be built for many years. The remaining three central terraces – Teviotdale, Dunrobin and Balmoral – were

14 The Colonies as they were in 1877, with the builders' yard in the centre.

15 An artist's impression of the builders' yard
as it may have looked in about 1895.

only partially built at first, because the builders' yard and workshops occupied the northern end of the ground. The first houses in all three of these terraces were started and finished at much the same time and by 1875 there were at least sixteen dwellings in each row. At the same time as these were being built, a row of houses and shops was under construction at Bridge Place (1872). Once again history was repeated, because building then switched back from the west to the east end. This was in 1875 when Keif House was remodelled and extended to make a total of six separate dwellings. It was then that the building was renamed Glenogle House, and Water Lane became Glenogle Road.

From 1875, building was sporadic as the three central terraces we gradually extended northwards. In Balmoral Place all but the last block of six houses was completed by the end of 1875, but the terrace wasn't finally finished until 1894 when the laundry at the river end was demolished. Similarly, Dunrobin and Teviotdale Places were built up in several stages, as the builders' yard and workshops were gradually taken down. By 1911, every available yard of ground had been built on, and the Park was complete.

16 The high-doors side of one of the terraces at Rosebank Cottages.

17 One of the four terraces of the Pilrig Model Buildings (now Shaw's Street).

THE BUILDINGS

Architecture

Apart from their regimented layout, the most distinctive feature of the Stockbridge Colonies, and other 'colonies' housing in Edinburgh, is the architecture. In a city otherwise dominated by tenements, town houses and villas, the cottage-style architecture of the colonies houses offers a striking contrast. But was it unique, and why was it chosen?

When the Cooperative started to build the Stockbridge Colonies in 1861, buildings of similar style already existed in the city. Of the two developments that were closest in design as well as aim, the earliest was at Pilrig, behind Leith Walk. Known then as the Pilrig Model Buildings (now Shaw's Place, Terrace and Street), these terraces were begun in 1849 and when complete provided rented homes for sixty-two families consisting of at least two rooms, access to a WC and a private garden. The upper dwellings were entered on the opposite side of the block from the ground floor houses by means of an internal staircase, and access to the front doors on both sides was provided by narrow paths running between the houses and their gardens.

The second development was started in the late 1850s and comprised three two-storey terraces with external staircases to provide access to the upper houses. Situated at Rosebank, off Gardener's Crescent, these houses were built by James Gowans, then a railway contractor but later Dean of Guild for the city and a pioneer of model dwellings for working people. There were thirty-six dwellings in this development, and each one had at least three rooms, a scullery and WC.

There is no doubt that the founders of the Cooperative would have been well aware of these earlier housing developments, indeed some of the first subscribers to the Cooperative were tenants at Pilrig and Rosebank. They may also have been aware that both these developments had met with some criticism from architects and social reformers alike. The houses at Pilrig were criticised for being 'not very substantially built', draughty, poorly ventilated and too small. Those at Rosebank were a definite improvement but still the rooms were small and cramped. Nevertheless, the houses were always fully let and certainly offered far better living conditions than could be found in most other buildings in the city.

The first houses to be built at Stockbridge owed much in their design to the two earlier developments, but they were generally a great improvement on what had gone before. Their construction was of better quality, the rooms were higher and larger in floor area and there was a greater distance between the terraces than at either Pilrig or Rosebank. Even so, the essential aim of all three developments was the same. As James Gowans put it, it was 'to get working men into small self-contained houses, where they would have their own door to go in by, every room being independent of the other having a door from the lobby for privacy, and having a little green attached to each house, and having everything arranged in a sanitary way....'.

The Pilrig Model Building Company and James Gowans had both employed architects to design their schemes – Patrick Wilson for Pilrig and Alexander MacGregor for Rosebank. But who, if anyone, was the architect for the Cooperative?

Unfortunately there are no records of an original plan or of the precise origin of the Colonies design, but there is an intriguing entry in the Company Minute Book for 1867 which provides a vital clue. The entry refers to an account for £9 19s 6d which was submitted to the Cooperative Management Committee by a recently retired Director named James Sutherland. Sutherland was an architect by profession, and one of the first people to buy a share in the Cooperative. His account was met with the following response – 'In respect, Mr Sutherland seems to have been under the impression that he was architect to the Company and would as such receive some remuneration for his professional assistance. The Directors, whilst distinctly denying that Mr Sutherland ever held this office, or was employed by them as such, yet agree to allow him £1. 1/– in full of the other items of his account.' It is also recorded in the Minutes that one of the Directors suggested that '10/- be allowed to the boy for the Paris Exhibition plans.' These were plans of the Cooperative's houses prepared for the Paris International Exhibition of 1867.

What these entries in the Minutes seem to suggest is that Sutherland did draw up some plans for the Company's houses, but the Directors assumed that his services would be voluntary. Whether or not Sutherland was responsible for the original design used at Reid Terrace is not clear, but as he was associated with the Cooperative right from the start, and was an architect, it seems very likely.

Once the basic design had been decided upon, the masons and other tradespeople would probably have worked out the details themselves. Only when a departure from this basic plan was considered did special plans have to be drawn. Judging from the Minutes, such plans were drawn by individual Directors, most of whom were joiners or masons rather than architects.

At Stockbridge, the basic model chosen for the houses was a two-story terrace comprising an average of sixteen dwellings on each level. As at Rosebank Cottages, the terraces rather than the streets were given a name and the houses were numbered in sequence, starting with the ground floor house at the main road end and ending with the upper house immediately above it but on the opposite side of the block. For visitors and newcomers to the area, this highly idiosyncratic system invariably causes confusion, and there can be few Colonies residents who have not, at some time or another, directed puzzled callers to 'the other side of the block'.

The most striking feature of the Colonies architecture is the external stone stairs leading to the upper ('high doors') houses on the opposite side from the ground floor ('low doors') houses. External stairs were already a common feature in some parts of Scotland. In Dundee, Perth, Cupar (Angus) and Stanley, for example, houses with external stairs existed before the Stockbridge Colonies were built, some with curved 'half-wheel' stairs and some with the stair at right angles to the houses. In many fishing communities, too, external 'forestairs' had long been a traditional feature, though they were mostly built parallel to the house wall rather than at right angles to it – as at Newhaven, for example. The reason for building external rather than internal staircases is not entirely clear, but it was probably partly to do with economics and partly tradition.

Amongst the advantages of this means of access were cost, privacy, and the saving of internal space. An outside staircase was cheaper to build than an internal stair, and used none of the precious floor area inside the house. The space beneath the external stairs was also an added bonus because it could be used for coal storage at ground level, thus keeping dust and dirt out of the house and saving the coalmen from an arduous climb. Indirectly, the stairs also served as garden walls and so offered a little privacy for the otherwise open and overlooked gardens. A commentator on the houses, writing in the 1860s, made the following observation:

18 These Victorian etchings of the high-door and low-door sides of two early Colonies terraces show how they must have looked when first built, with wooden garden fences, iron clothes poles and railings on the stairs and low walls next to the main road.

'The arrangement of separate entrances on opposite sides struck me as being an exceedingly novel yet simple contrivance for securing absolute completeness and privacy to the occupants of the two parts of the tenement, and for solving the difficulty of providing house-room for two families under the same roof, without the possibility of their interfering with each other's comfort, or even coming into each other's way, and yet giving to each family its own garden with a different roadway in front.'

Internally, the arrangement of the rooms shows a number of variations between houses of different date and location, but the original model chosen at Stockbridge comprised a kitchen with bed recess, sink and range; a large parlour with a fireplace; a small bedroom, and a WC and coal cellar. The upper houses generally had an additional two bedrooms in the attics and both upper and lower houses had access to a 20 x 17 foot garden and a communal drying and bleaching green. The Reid Terrace houses were built to this design, though some of the upper houses lacked made-up attics and none of them had dormer windows. Small dormers were first introduced on the high-doors side of Hugh Miller Place and all but a handful of houses in later terraces were fitted with slightly larger versions.

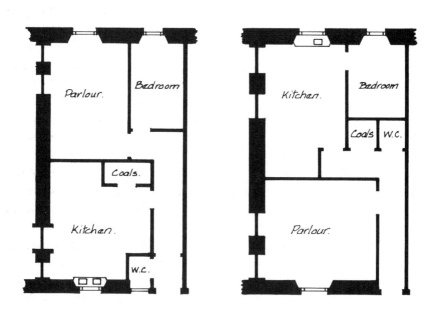

19 Plans to show two of the many different designs
for ground floor Colonies houses.

The building of the bulk of the houses spanned just over a decade and in that time several variations were introduced to the original design. Oriel (or bay) windows were first tried out at 15 Collins Place and later built on houses in Avondale, Teviotdale, Dunrobin and Glenogle Places. Where there was extra space at the river end, as at Avondale and Kemp Places, larger, double-fronted houses were built and at Glenogle Terrace internal stairs were introduced for the first time.

Between the first and second phases of building, there was a gap of over ten years and it was during that time (in 1879) that the jurisdiction of the Dean of Guild was extended to include the Stockbridge area. It was the task of the City Council's Dean of Guild to check and approve all building plans and to make recommendations for changes and improvements. When in 1883 the Cooperative submitted its standard house plan for approval, it met with some criticism from the Dean of Guild who commented on the lack of ventilation for the WCs and on the poor siting of the kitchen sinks in small cupboards, instead of under the windows. It was almost certainly as a result of these criticisms that the Cooperative decided to amend the original plans to include bathrooms in the last houses to be built in Dunrobin, Balmoral and Teviotdale Places.

Although the decision regarding house design rested entirely in the hands of the Company's Management Committee, members of the Committee were always prepared to consider modifications to their basic plans if potential purchasers requested them. The most obvious example of such a request being met is the case of Glenogle Place. According to the Company Minutes, some of the people who had expressed interest in the proposed terrace had asked for the houses to be 'a little superior to the present ones', as compensation for their being sited parallel to the main road. James Colville obviously felt that such a request should be met since it would improve the Company's chances of making a sale. Accordingly, David Bell (a Director) drew sketches for houses of slightly different design and these were approved and used.

The area of design in which house buyers had most freedom of choice was that of internal fittings and finishes. By paying extra money, buyers could be supplied with special fittings by the Company. This 'jobbing work' provided the Cooperative with a little extra income and gave house owners the opportunity to add distinctive details to their own homes. There are no written records of requests for internal variations, but given the evidence of the houses themselves, it is likely that ceiling mouldings and fireplaces were the features which tended to be 'customised' most often. Probably the most striking example of this 'customising' of detail is to be seen at 32 Bell Place which has a particularly elaborate ceiling moulding in the sitting room and a set of beautiful iron balconies on both sides of the house. It is probably no coincidence

20 Number 32 Bell Place, home of the Colville family from 1867 to 1886.

that this house first belonged to James Colville who, as Manager of the Cooperative, may have been offered these embellishments free of charge.

Despite these variations to internal details and design, the Colonies houses must have presented an almost uniform appearance when they were first built. The building stone was from local sandstone quarries and was laid and dressed in the same style in all the terraces. The slates, too, were of uniform colour on all roofs except Reid Terrace, and even the lime for the mortar came from one source – Burdiehouse. Every garden had its own pair of line posts and was bounded by either a standard wooden fence or a wall topped with iron railings. And then there was the most unifying feature of all – the regulation green paintwork.

No discussion of the Colonies architecture would be complete without some reference to the much celebrated plaques on the gable ends of Collins, Balmoral, Dunrobin, Teviotdale, Avondale and Kemp Places. Collins Place was the first to be adorned with sculptures, and carries the commemorative plaque, the Company symbol and a carved head (see page 54). The pairs of plaques on the other five terraces depict the tools of a wide variety of trades including joiner, mason, decorator, plumber and plasterer. All these trades were represented amongst the membership of the Cooperative, but there does not appear to be any significance in the siting of the plaques on particular terraces.

Labour and materials

During the ten or so years when most of the Stockbridge Colonies houses were being built, the Cooperative was also building houses on at least five other sites in Edinburgh and Leith (Ferry Road, Hawthorn Bank, Dalry Road, Easter Road, Restalrig – see map 2). The Company's demand for labour and materials was never as great as it was in that first decade. The number of employees is said to have reached 250 during that period, and in 1871 there were 48 joiners, 41 stonemasons, 25 labourers, 20 plasterers, 5 plumbers, one carter, one blacksmith, one clerk, and the Manager. The work which could not be done by the Company's own employees was put out to tender and, in general, the firms that gave the lowest estimates were the ones selected for the job. The tradespeople employed on this basis included lathers, glaziers, ironmongers, slaters and mantelpiece makers. For those people fortunate enough to be employed by the Cooperative, wages were generally good and even a little higher than the rates offered elsewhere. Masons were the highest paid (6¾d per hour), then joiners (6¼d) . In 1866, the foreman joiner earned 31/- a week which was 9/- less than James Colville, the Manager.

Because of the general nature of the Company records, it is difficult to be precise about the sources of building materials used at Glenogle Road. At least five different quarries are listed as sources of building stone (Craigleith, Redhall,

21 Although the setting for this photograph of stonemasons is Comrie, not Stockbridge, the scene is probably very similar to one that might have been seen at Stockbridge in the 1870s.

Hailes, Ravelston and Dunmore) of which all except Dunmore (near Stirling) were within a few miles of the Colonies site at Stockbridge. In each case, the stone produced was good quality sandstone and varied from grey to reddish pink in colour. Judging from the appearance and finish of the Colonies houses, most of the stone must have come from the Craigleith and Ravelston quarries, and most of the roof slates from Ballachulish. The latter arrived by ship at Leith Docks.

THE ORIGIN OF THE NAME 'COLONIES'

The term 'colony' has a number of different meanings, one of which is 'a community of people of the same nationality or pursuits concentrated in a particular place (e.g. an artists' colony)'. Given that the Stockbridge and other 'colonies' were built to house working people, or artisans, they clearly fit this definition, each being, in effect, an 'artisans' colony'. Add to this the distinctive clustered layout and unusual architecture of the houses, and it is clear why the term 'colonies' came to be used as a descriptive term.

Another use of the term 'colony' is to describe a hive of bees, and it is interesting that the Cooperative chose the image of a bee hive surrounded by bees as a Company seal which was used on official documents during the early years. The bee hive image also appears on carved stone plaques on two of the Cooperative's colonies terraces (see Figure 22). The same image was adopted by the labour movement in the nineteenth century to symbolise a community, or colony, of workers and the notion of worker cooperation, and in 1861, a weekly newspaper called *The Beehive* was founded by George Potter 'in the interests of the working classes'. Clearly, the founders of the Cooperative were much in sympathy with the ideals and aims of the labour movement and did much to further its cause – hence their decision to adopt the bee hive symbol.

In Edinburgh, it is common for people to speak of 'colonies-type housing' to describe terraces of two-storey stone houses laid out parallel to one another, and even to describe houses which, though not arranged in parallel terraces nevertheless have an upper and a lower dwelling, each with its own front door (as at Glendevon Place, for example). Although most of these so-called 'colonies' were built by the Edinburgh Cooperative Building Company, some – such as the houses off Industrial Road beside Leith Links – were not. However, most people when asked what they mean by Edinburgh's 'colonies' will refer to the Cooperative's houses at Stockbridge, Dalry, Abbeyhill, Slateford Road and Restalrig because it is these that fit the basic model.

As mentioned earlier, and illustrated by map 2, the Cooperative did in fact build on many more sites around the city, and, in one case – along part of what is now Ferry Road but was originally known as Henderson Place/Trafalgar

22 This stone bee hive plaque is on the wall of Lewis Terrace in the Dalry Road Colonies. A similar plaque appears on the gable end of Myrtle Terrace at North Merchiston Park.

Street – they departed from the Stockbridge model and built tenements instead. This is particularly surprising, given that, in a Company prospectus of around 1920, the Cooperative describes itself as 'a pioneer in providing for those who prefer the privacy of self-contained dwellings with private gardens to houses in common stair tenements'.

In summary, then, there are clear reasons why the term 'colonies' came into use as a general descriptive term to describe houses of like kind which stood out from the rest because of their unusual appearance and layout. What is interesting, however, is that despite the fact that the Cooperative gave a name to each of its main developments, these names are not now used. In the case of the Stockbridge Colonies, the name Glenogle Park was carved on a stone plaque on the wall of Collins Place (see Figure 12) and was used as part of the address by the Cooperative on its official documents. For example, James Colville gave his address as 32 Bell Place, Glenogle Park, and the builder's yard as Balmoral Place, Glenogle Park. Most of the other colonies developments were also given names – Norton Park for the Abbeyhill houses, Shaftesbury Park for those at Slateford, Restalrig Park for those at Leith, and so on. The names have not persisted however, and even people who have lived in these areas for over 70 years and whose parents and grandparents lived there before them do not use these names. One reason, perhaps, is that they were too grandiose for the cottage-style houses – the term 'Park' being more suitable for a garden city development than for artisan's houses.

In the case of Stockbridge, where the houses have long been known as The Colonies, it can only be assumed that this is because they were the first development of this kind and so took the prefix 'The' to denote a place name rather than a descriptive term.

Street History

OWNERS AND OCCUPIERS

The Tables in the Appendix list the names and occupations of the first people to own and to live in each of the houses in the Colonies. A quick glance at these soon shows that the pattern of owner-occupation varied amongst the terraces. In some, the majority of the house owners were also the occupiers; in others the majority of the houses were let. Colville and Kemp Places had the highest ratio of owner-occupiers to tenants (23:7) and Hugh Miller Place had the reverse, with twenty-six tenanted houses and only six owner-occupied. Overall, the numbers were nearly equal, with about ten more owner-occupied houses than tenanted ones

An even closer study of the Tables reveals that certain individuals owned more than one house, and in some cases the owners did not themselves live in the Colonies. The most glaring example of this is in Hugh Miller Place where Mr James Ross, a photographer living in West Powderhall, owned and let a total of twenty-four houses. It is because of discoveries such as these that some writers have criticised the Cooperative for what seemed to be absentee landlordism on a grand scale. 'So much for the cooperative ideal' they have said, and 'what about the desire to make "every man his own landlord"?' Certainly, the evidence of the Tables is that 'every man' was not 'his own landlord', but what they do show is that the people who lived in the houses were genuine working people, nearly all employed in manual trades.

Although all the references so far have been to male house owners and tenants, as the Tables show, there were also several female house owners who were 'heads of households' either because they were single parents, widows, or unmarried and living alone.

Without records of the rents paid, it is not possible to tell if the tenants were unfairly charged or not, but it is highly unlikely since the Cooperative Manager and Directors went to great pains to ensure that all house buyers were fully in sympathy with the Cooperative cause. It is quite possible, therefore, that James Ross paid his £3440 for twenty-four houses in Hugh Miller Place as a gesture of goodwill towards the new venture. There is no doubt that a lump sum of that size would have done a great deal to boost the Company's funds at a time when income was uncertain, and Mr Ross would have had to wait many years before his investment was paid off by income from annual rents. Even if he had chosen to resell the houses, he would have made very little profit since their value remained static for many decades.

CHANGING PATTERNS OF LIVING

There are many people aged above sixty living in the Colonies today, and a high proportion of them have lived in the area most or all of their lives. Some still live in houses which have been owned and lived in by their families for two or even three generations; others live in houses which they bought for themselves after leaving the original Colonies family home. As a result of this continuity from one generation to the next, memories of the Colonies go back over a century or more to when the houses were still being built.

One of the most common and vivid memories of the past is of the large numbers of children who lived, played and went to school together. As some of the photographs in this section show, there were many more children living in the streets in the 1920s, '40s and '50s than there are nowadays, but even at the turn of the century the numbers were quite small compared with the 1880s. The 1881 Census reveals that some Colonies streets housed as many as seventy and even eighty children under the age of sixteen, giving an average per street of fifty-five children. This compares with an average in 1978 of only six children per street. In that year there were only seventy-nine children under sixteen in the whole Colonies community, compared with 671 nearly a century earlier.

A more detailed picture of the way the size of the community has changed is shown in the Table on page 42 where figures for the years 1881 and 1978 are compared. Apart from the change in the overall population size, the most remarkable feature shown up in the Table is the change in size of the average household, from about six or seven people per house to only two. In the 1880s, and for some time after, it was common to find two parents and six children living in five or even three rooms. One upper house in Collins Place (number 25) was recorded as housing a family of eleven people in 1881, comprising the father aged fifty-two, the mother aged forty-six, and their nine children ranging in age from two to twenty-four. It is small wonder that with families of such a size, the upper houses were the most sought after, and not surprising that families often moved from the smaller, ground floor houses into upper ones as the number of children grew.

This movement from one house to another was quite common, as was the tendency for successive generations to continue to live in the Colonies. A good example of both these patterns of living is shown by the Colville family who first moved into the Colonies two years after James was elected Manager of the Cooperative. James and his wife, Elizabeth Robb, and their children Andrew,

Isabella, Catherine, Elizabeth and Susan, all moved into the newly built Hugh Miller Cottage in 1863 and stayed there until 1867 when they bought a larger house at 32 Bell Place. Apart from wanting more space for the growing children, James and Elizabeth probably felt that a larger, grander house was more fitting for the Company Manager and his family. Their next and final move was in 1886, the year that James was elected a Justice of the Peace. By now a man of some standing in the city as well as the local community, it was entirely fitting that he and his wife, two daughters and a granddaughter should move into the upper half of the first double fronted house to be built in the Colonies, at 16 Kemp Place. With a total of eight good-sized rooms, and a river-end location, this was probably the most desirable house in the Colonies at the time.

As Manager of the Cooperative, James Colville was obviously better placed than anyone to buy Colonies property at the lowest prices, and he must have taken every opportunity to do so because by the time of his death in 1892 he owned a total of fifteen houses in the community. His daughter Isabella had moved into one of them (30 Avondale Place) when she married, and she and her surviving sisters, niece and nephew inherited the rest when James died. For many years Elizabeth Colville and her niece Jane continued to live at 16 Kemp Place, then Jane moved into 1 Bridge Place where she lived alone for a time before moving out of the Colonies altogether. Living alone or with sisters or brothers was quite common at that time, but there were far fewer single-

23 A group of children from the 'east end' of the Colonies, taken about 1920, next to Glenogle Place.

24 Local children posing on Gabriel's Steps (the 'dummy steps') in 1920.

25 Taken in about 1940, this photograph shows Colonies children who lived in two or three terraces around Avondale/Kemp Place (where the photograph was taken). The number of children here represents half the total number living in the whole of the Colonies in 1978!

person households in the Colonies in the early 1900s than there are now. As the Table on page 42 shows, by 1978 is was quite common to find ten or more single-person households in each street (and even more common in the late 1990s), whereas the average was only one or two in 1881.

Looking back over the century or more since the first Colonies houses were built, the changes have been quite dramatic. Not only has the population shrunk from a peak of over 2000 in the 1880s to less than a third of that figure, the community has changed from being one dominated by large families to one dominated by single-person or two-person households. Also, what was once a relatively uniform population is now one which is thoroughly mixed in terms of ages, occupations, incomes and lifestyles. As one elderly resident put it in 1993:

'The neighbours all used to know each other. I don't know who stays in the first house here now – no idea. Everything was more neighbourly then...we were brought up that if there's anything you can do for anybody, it's your duty to do it – get on with it. And I think all the families were brought up that way. That's changing. And of course people are busier now, they're out working, the wife, the mother, too. There's not the same time. There's no time for neighbourliness. The mothers are out working and when they come back they've the shopping and the housework to do.'

Changes of this kind are obviously not unique to the Colonies but are typical of the population as a whole over the same period. What is more unusual, however, is the way in which the value of the houses has changed over that period. For the first two or three decades, the selling prices of the houses remained more or less the same as they had been when first built. For example, James Colville bought 16 Kemp Place for exactly the same sum (£250) in 1886 as the first buyer had paid in 1868. By 1946, the same house was sold again for £600, and not until the 1960s did the price rise above the £1000 mark. From the late 1960s onwards, the value of all the houses rose steeply and dramatically, and by the early 1980s 'modernised' upper houses were selling for as much as £40 000. By the mid-1990s, upper houses were regularly being sold for over £90 000, and in 1997, figures of over £100 000 were not uncommon. Even accounting for inflation, such a steep increase is remarkable, especially for houses which were not long ago described as 'a poor class of property' by a then Director of E. B. Contractors – the Company that started life as The Edinburgh Cooperative Building Company.

Public regard for the Colonies houses must still have been quite low as recently as 1966, because it was in that year that a plan was proposed whereby some of them would be demolished to make way for a new Inner City Ring Road, part of which was to follow the course of the Water of Leith where it runs beside the Colonies. Not surprisingly, the proposal appalled the Colonies residents who promptly formed their own Association in order to raise money to pay legal costs for the fight against the Ring Road. Enough money was eventually raised by the Colonies, partly by holding a Colonies summer fête (now a regular community event), and the fight won. It may have been as an indirect result of this dispute that the Colonies houses were later declared List B buildings, thus becoming protected against future demolition and damaging alterations in appearance as well as being rightly recognised as buildings of intrinsic architectural and historical interest. Such recognition is a great tribute not only to the imaginative design and quality of building, but to the courage and vision of the pioneering cooperative artisans.

Number of:	Dwellings (E=1 empty)		People		Children under 16		People over 60		Single-person households	
STREETS	1881	1978	1881	1978	1881	1978	1881	1978	1881	1978
Reid (U), Bridge Place	28(E)	25(E)	151	50	57	5	1	8	2	9
Reid (L), Hugh Miller (L)	36(E)	35	170	45	62	0	6	18	0	24
Hugh Miller (U & cott.), Rintoul (U)	33	33(E)	181	72	70	15	9	12	2	3
Rintoul (L), Colville (L)	31	31	133	50	38	0	5	14	1	15
Colville (U), Collins (L)	30	30	161	65	48	8	12	6	1	10
Collins (L), Balmoral (U)	27	30(E)	132	50	55	2	8	18	1	13
Balmoral (L), Dunrobin (U)	20	30(E)	109	57	49	8	5	21	0	13
Dunrobin (L), Teviotdale (U)	16	30	80	63	28	11	8	14	4	9
Teviotdale (L), Avondale (U)	23	31	144	67	59	10	2	14	2	11
Avondale (L), Kemp (U)	31	32	151	61	57	4	5	15	1	10
Kemp (L), Bell (U)	31	31(E)	165	65	65	12	10	8	0	9
Bell (L), Glenogle Place, Terrace, House	38	38	191	68	83	4	8	19	1	13
totals	344	376	1768	713	671	79	79	167	15	139
averages	28 per street	31	147 per street	59	55 per street 38% of total pop.	6 11% of total pop.	4% of total pop.	23%	4% of total dwellings	37%

Table of housing statistics for the years 1881 and 1978 – Stockbridge Colonies

26 This aerial photograph of the Stockbridge Colonies was taken in the early 1980s.

Appendix

In the pages that follow, the Colonies terraces are looked at in the order in which they were built, rather than their order on the ground. For each terrace, there are general notes for which most of the information was culled from the Cooperative's Minute Books, and there are owner/occupier Tables compiled from Valuation Rolls. The Tables list the names and occupations of the first people to own and to live in each house. Because of the time interval between the building of the terraces, some names appear in more than one Table, either because occupiers moved from older to newer houses, or because owners of early houses went on to buy more recent ones.

Where names or occupations are missing from some Tables, this is because they were not listed in the original Rolls, or else were indecipherable.

27 Collins/Balmoral Places as they were in about 1902. The iron railings on top of the walls were removed to make munitions in the 1940s, and the gas lights in the streets were later replaced by electric lights.

Reid Terrace

Why so named?: In honour of Hugh Gilzean Reid, who along with James Colville, 'founded' the Edinburgh Cooperative Building Company in 1861 (see page 12). Reid was a typical self-made man. Born in Cruden in 1836, he was the son of a shoemaker and farmer, and his mother was an ardent supporter of the Free Church cause. He made his way up in the field of journalism, and moved to Edinburgh in the late 1850s to become editor of the *Edinburgh Weekly News*. It was during his three-year stay in the city that he became a passionate campaigner for social and industrial reform and, in particular, for the nine-hour day. Although only twenty-four at the time, he was able to do much to help James Colville and his fellow masons to turn the cooperative idea into reality and used the pages of his newspaper to promote the new Company as widely as possible. For many years after leaving Edinburgh, Reid kept in contact with the Cooperative, and wrote and spoke widely of its successes. His book, *Housing the People: An Example in Cooperation* described the origins and early years of the Cooperative and is something of a classic of its type.

Reid and his wife and their twelve children spent most of their lives in the Birmingham area of England where, in 1886, Reid was elected as Liberal MP in Gladstone's government. As an MP and public figure, he continued to fight for improvements in the living and working conditions of working people, and it was partly because of this, as well as his successes in the newspaper industry, that he was knighted in 1893. Three years before that he became President of the Institute of Journalists, and in 1904, seven years before he died, Sir Hugh was elected the first President of the World's Press Parliament.

Date when building began: October 1861

Original selling price of the houses: £130 for ground floor, and £150 for upper floor houses with made-up attics.

Notes, and features of interest: The first terrace to be built by the Edinburgh Cooperative Building Company, and the only one in the Colonies built without dormer (oriel) windows in the attic floor, and with continuous window sills and small upper windows alternating with larger ones.

The foundation stone was laid by The Reverend James Begg (see page 23) who placed a bottle in the cavity of the stone containing several coins, copies of local newspapers, a copy of the laws and contracts of the Company, a list of its shareholders and a statement of its origins.

Number 4 was first owned and lived in for many years by Mrs Agnes Hamill who ran a greengrocer's shop there. James Duff Brown and his family lived next door to Mrs Hamill, at number 3, and James recalls her in his childhood memoirs, as follows:

'My earliest recollections are quite clear, and one of them concerns a tumble I had down a ladder into a vegetable cellar in the garden of Mrs Hamill, who was a greengrocer and our next door neighbour, at No. 4 Reid Terrace. She was the first to rescue me from my fall and comfort me with acid drops! This old lady had an old-fashioned mangle, a huge long box weighted with stones, which ran over rollers and thus pressed out the clothes. It was worked by a wheel-handle and many a pin of clothes I helped to mangle in after years.'

REID TERRACE: OWNERS/OCCUPIERS

No.	Owner	Occupation	Tenant	Occupation
1	D. Berwick	mason		
2	R. Hunter	glasscutter		
3	G. Coutts Douglas	lathsplitter	J. Duff Brown	
4	Mrs Hamill			
5	W. Carruthers	engineer	H.P. Thorne	clerk
6	R McWilliams			
7	G. Ross	letter carrier		
8	W. Peebles	tailor		
9	A. J. Kilgour	watchmaker		
10	J. Currie	labourer		
11	W. White	shoemaker		
12	A. Topping	joiner		
13	J. Ritchie	glasscutter		
14	Mrs Miller			
15	J. Macdonald	jeweller	J. Hay	saddler
16	R. Somerville	stationer	P. Gloag	clerk
17	J. Dobbie	vandriver		
18	W. Wighton	watchmaker	J. Dawson	gardener
19	W. Wilson	jeweller	W. Nicholson	clerk
20	as above		Mrs Scott	
21	as above		J. Brown	confectioner
22	as above		D. Horne	clerk of works

23	W. Wighton	watchmaker	G. Horne	hairdresser
24	J. Mackay	watchmaker		
25	Miss MacGregor			
26	J. MacDonald	jeweller	J. Gilbertson	glazier
27	Mrs Paterson		J. Gibb	railway servant
28	Miss Ritchie		Mrs Forbes	
29	Mrs M. Purdie		G. Scott	traveller
30	A. Hall	pocketbook maker		
31	C. Grierson			
32	J. Hunter	GPO sorter	R. Cromb	clerk
33	R. Hay	shop porter	J. Mackay	watchmaker
34	P. Burt	shop porter	J. Kennedy	plasterer
35	A. Sawers	blacksmith		
36	C. Lyon	hosier		
37	S. Adam	skinner		
38	J. Ritchie	glasscutter	A. Dougal	bootmaker
39	A. Garland	glasscutter	L. Minck	watch & clock maker
40	C. Shutt	servant		

Hugh Miller Place

Why so named?: As a tribute to Hugh Miller; a fellow stonemason and champion of the cause for housing reform (see page 11). It is a great sadness that Miller was not alive to record the event because he would undoubtedly have had something to say on the subject either in the pages of *The Witness* newspaper (which he edited) or in one of his celebrated essays.

Before his suicide in 1856, he had written much on the subject of the need for better dwellings for working people, but he had also spoken out about the 'uncivilised' nature of many a stonemason and the 'absurdity' of giving the working man the vote. What he would have made of this new venture into home-ownership by artisans can only be guessed at, but it is likely that he would have regarded it with optimism rather than alarm.

Date when building began: 1862

Notes, and features of interest: This, the second terrace to be built, was the only one to have a small cottage at the road end. This was first used as a house (by the Colville family), but later converted into two shops and finally one, with a small flat above.

Perhaps the most interesting feature of this terrace is its history of ownership (see Table and page 36), it being the first and only one in which the majority of the houses were sold to one buyer. Sadly, there are no records remaining of the discussions that must have taken place before this sale was completed, but it seems highly probable that the buyer, James Ross, was either well acquainted with one of the Directors of the Cooperative, or with one of its promoters. All the houses that he bought were immediately let to artisan tenants, and continued to be let out for many years before being sold off individually.

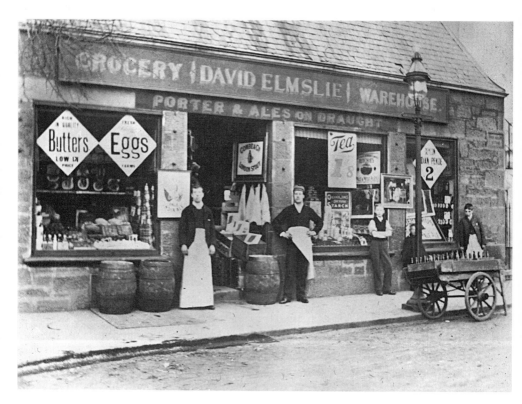

28 Elmslie's shop occupied Hugh Miller Cottage
in the early 1890s, when this picture was taken.

HUGH MILLER PLACE: OWNERS/OCCUPIERS

No.	Owner	Occupation	Tenant	Occupation
1	J. Ross	photographer	M. Veitch	railway clerk
2	as above		J. Soutter	ironmonger
3	as above		R. Bain	clerk
4	as above		S. Yarrol	furrier
5	as above		G. Fulton	gardener
6	as above		G. Rodimer	gardener
7	as above		J. Wilson Horne	teacher
8	as above		J. Gregory	silversmith
9	as above		Miss I. Moffat	
10	as above		D. Reid Grubb	clerk
11	as above		W. McEvoy	clerk, stamp office
12	as above		J. Walker	servant
13	G. Lennox	miller	A. Thomson	railway guard
14	T. Early	drill instructor		
15	G. Furmage	butler		
16	A. Smith	coachman		
17	W. Gray	blacksmith	Mrs Wright	
18	D. Turner	clerk		
19	J. Kennedy	plasterer		
20	W. Aitken	collector		
21	J. Ross	photographer	D. Clerk	
22	as above		R. Brown	bootmaker
23	as above		A. Harper	servant
24	as above		G. Matheson	GPO stamper
25	as above		C. Barnett	smith
26	as above		W. Milne	warehouse man
27	as above		J. Riddle	glazier
28	as above		A. Gillespie	shopman
29	as above		G. Wright	bathkeeper
30	as above		A. Wood	mason
31	as above		W. Brownlee	draper
32	as above		W. Wetherston	flesher
Hugh Miller Cottage	J. Colville	mason		

Rintoul Place

Why so named?: As a compliment to David Rintoul, one of the seven masons who became the first subscribers to the Edinburgh Cooperative Building Company and co-signatories of the original document of registration. Rintoul was elected first Chairman of the Cooperative and was re-elected for the year 1870-1871. He remained a Director for many years and lived in Reid Terrace for a time.

Date when building began: 1863

Original selling price of the houses: Not known, but since all the upper houses had dormer windows, it is likely that the price for these was a little over £150.

Notes, and features of interest: Amongst the first people to buy houses in this terrace, there were several multiple house owners, some of whom already owned property in the two earlier terraces, and others who went on to buy houses in later terraces. For example, Charles Shutt (No. 2) already owned and lived in 40 Reid Terrace, and Mrs Margaret Purdie (wife of George Purdie, an engine driver with the Eastern Bengal Railway Company) already owned 29 Reid Terrace and went on to buy houses in Colville and Collins Places, in addition to the one at 6 Rintoul Place. Samuel Yarrol, a furrier and ostrich feather maker, who first lived at No. 5, later moved to 1 Glenogle Place when it was first built, and also bought six other houses in the Colonies. George Furmage at No. 24 already owned and lived in 15 Hugh Miller Place, and Alexander Calder (No. 8) bought six houses in Avondale Place and moved into one of them (No. 15) where he lived until his death.

RINTOUL PLACE: OWNERS/OCCUPIERS

No.	Owner	Occupation	Tenant	Occupation
1	T. Black	mason		
2	C. Shutt	servant	W. Pagan	
3	Mrs Elder			
4	J. Smith	mason		
5	S. Yarroll	furrier		
6	Mrs Purdle		J. Scott	clerk
7	D. Pitt	butler		
8	A. Calder	sculptor		
9	G. Scott	traveller		

10	D. Gibb	joiner		
11	Mrs Purdie		Mrs Ewart	
12	J. Dall	joiner		
13	N. Heggie	woodcutter	D. Ireland	teacher
14	J. Orr Burns		J. Black	shopman
15	J. Bruce	gardener		
16	P. Ashcroft	glasscutter		
17	J. Johnston	coachman		
18	J. McDougall	teacher		
19	G. Hendrie	butler	W. Palmer	saddler
20	P. Lyle			
21	J. Miller	joiner		
22	W. Dall	house painter		
23	W. Hannah	dentist		
24	G. Furmage	butler	J. Orchadson	tailor
25	Mrs C. Campbell		D. Weir	egg merchant
26	J. Lamb	carver & gilder	Miss Smith	
27	D. Bell	joiner		
28	J. Taylor	Gov. Edin. Prison	M. Rae	
29	R Crombe	law clerk		
30	J. Spence	painter	(vacant)	
31	J. Affleck	pavier		
32	J. Archibald	stationer		

Colville Place

Why so named?: In honour of James Colville, a stonemason and co-founder of the Edinburgh Cooperative Building Company for which he served as Manager from its beginning in 1861 until his retirement in 1889 (see page 13). Colville must have been a man of remarkable energy and ability, since it was he who, more or less single-handedly, ran the day-to-day business of the Company during its busiest and most successful years. His job involved an enormous amount of walking each day; from home to the Company office in the centre of town, to all the various building sites, and to visit lawyers, feu superiors etc. It is no wonder, therefore, that in 1867 he made the following request to the Management Committee – 'in connection with the business of the Company I have a very great deal of walking, and suggest for the consideration of the Directors the propriety of allowing me a small pony and gig for my use.'

James Colville had five children and outlived all but three of them. He lived in the Colonies from 1863 until his death from 'lung congestion and asthma' at the age of 70. By that time, he owned as many as fifteen houses in the Colonies, all of which were left to his family, some of whom continued to live in them for many years. In 1886, he was elected a JP by the recently retired Lord Provost, George Harrison, thus becoming the first 'workman' magistrate of the city.

Date when building began: Probably 1865

Original selling price of houses:

Notes, and features of interest: The only street in which two adjacent ground floor houses were owned and occupied by one person (see Table). The owner, Peter Hume, may have had a large family and so bought both houses to accommodate them all, or he may even have used both houses as one, with access between the two inside.

COLVILLE PLACE: OWNERS/OCCUPIERS

No.	Owner	Occupation	Tenant	Occupation
1	P. Hume	inspector of lighthouses		
2	*As above*			
3	W. Milne	warehouseman		
4	R. Thomson	sculptor		
5	A. Lawson	mason		
6	W. Worthington		J. Scott	clerk
7	A. Fraser		J. Auchincloss	smith
8	R. Foster	plasterer		
9	J. Porteous	upholsterer		
10	E. Douglas	joiner		
11	D. Lockhart	compositor		
12	W. Simpson	warehouseman		
13	R. Davidson		P. Forbes	clerk
14	W. Tait	cabinetmaker		
15	Mrs Miller			
16	C. Drye			
17	J. Cowan	mason		
18	H. Swanson	bank clerk	J. Ramsay	bookseller

19	W. Lochart	gardener	Mrs Mitchell	
20	Mrs Purdie		D. Louden	dock labourer
21	Miss C. Dawson		J. Dawson	joiner
22	J. Keppie	printer		
23	G. Morton	joiner		
24	T. Dunkel	waiter		
25	C. Romanes			
26	C. McKay	policeman		
27	A. Simpson	cabinetmaker		
28	G. Matheson	GPO stamper		
29	A. Wood	mason		
30	G. Sime	blacksmith		

Collins Place

Why so named?: James Collins was elected Chairman of the Cooperative for the year 1866-1867, hence the choice of his name for this terrace, most of which was built during the same year. Collins was a stonemason by trade, and one of the seven who became the first subscribers to the Cooperative. He was also a prominent member of the Edinburgh Trades Council, for which he had acted as treasurer for over six years, and was one-time President of the Masons' Union.

Date when building began: 1866

Original selling price of the houses: Not known except for the two river-end houses with bay windows, of which the ground floor was £215 and the upper, £265.

Notes, and features of interest: This was the last terrace to be built at the west end for some years, and the one chosen to carry a carved plaque commemorating the start of building operations on the Colonies site (see page 22). The name 'Glenogle Park' which appears on this plaque was probably chosen as a gesture of goodwill towards the Haig family, since James Richard Haig, one of the heirs to the land, then lived at Glenogle (or Glenogil) in Forfarshire. The other gable-end features of this terrace are the carved head, and the dated, sculpted arch stone above the lower window. According to the Company Minutes, the stone was to depict the Company seal, but the actual seal found on various Company documents depicts a bee hive surrounded by bees (see pages 34-35). The identity of the carved head is not recorded in the Minutes, but some sources suggest it is Hugh Gilzean Reid and others that it is James Collins.

The river-end block has an extra three feet of ground attached, and it was because of this that the Directors decided to choose the end houses to 'trial the cost' of building oriel (bay) windows onto the sitting rooms.

As the Table shows, number 1 Collins Place was owned in the first year by James Colville's son, Andrew.

29 The Edinburgh Cooperative's seal and the sculpted head
on the gable end of Collins Place.

COLLINS PLACE: OWNERS/OCCUPIERS

No.	Owner	Occupation	Tenant	Occupation
1	A. Colville	printer	R. Laing	clerk
2	Miss J. McLauchlan		G. Mill	clerk
3	R. Blaikie	gardener		
4	G. Spence	mason	J. Craig	compositor
5	S. Yarroll	furrier	J. Wilson	clerk
6	*As above*		J. Goodwillie	clerk
7	A. Ross	mason		
8	W. Davidson	joiner		
9	A. Aitken	cabinetmaker		
10	W. Gourlay	mason		
11	T. Early	drill instructor	P. Robertson	clerk
12	*As above*		A. McKechnie	mason
13	J. Bishop	compositor		

14	Mrs Purdie	student			
15	J. Scott				
16	Mrs Kinniburgh				
17	Mrs Purdie		G. Bird	clerk	
18	R. Coull	china merchant	J. Meldrum	draper	
19	T. Early	drill instructor	J. Donald	gardener	
20	*As above*		G. Croall	piano tuner	
21	J. Austin	butler			
22	J. Anderson	printer			
23	O. Johnston	sculptor			
24	A. McColl	warehouseman			
25	J. Brown	tea merchant	R. Jamieson	coachsmith	
26	G. Johnson	bootmaker	J. Matthews	goldsmith	
27	T. Peddie	civil engineer			
28	W. Donald	dyer			
29	J. Dempster	commercial trav.			
30	R. Cunningham	cabinetmaker	D. Lynn	cabinetmaker	

Bell Place

Why so named?: In honour of David Bell, a joiner and the elected Chairman of the Cooperative for the years 1867-1869. Bell had been a Director and member of the Management Committee before becoming Chairman, and he was also one of the three or four Directors who drew up plans for some of the early houses such as those in Glenogle Place and at Dalry Road. He resigned before the end of his term of office to start up his own building business.

Date when building began: 1867

Notes, and features of interest: Number 32 was the home of the Colville family for many years (see pages 32 and 37). This is almost certainly the reason for the special architectural features such as the iron balconies, wide window and door architraves, bay gable-end window and elaborate ceiling mouldings.

The wooden footbridge at the end of Bell Place was built in 1894 at a total cost (including footpaths) of £453.13s, and paid for by the Town Council. The builder was John Morris and Sons.

30 The wooden footbridge at the end of Bell Place.

BELL PLACE: OWNERS/OCCUPIERS

No.	Owner	Occupation	Tenant	Occupation
1	S. Yarroll	furrier	G. Nicol	shoemaker
2	A. Scott	plumber	J. Milne	
3	J. Brown	sculptor		
4	R. Proudfoot	gilder		
5	W. Palmer	saddler	W. Wright	clerk
6	J. Purves	joiner		
7	G. Dickson	joiner		
8	J. Wilson	traveller		
9	Mrs Anderson			
10	Miss D. Smith		W. Edwards	clerk
11	A. Home	grocer		
12	G. Cation	joiner		
13	R. Donald	reporter	R. Alexander	painter
14	*As above*		Miss I. Greig	
15	A. Greenlaw	cabinetmaker		
16	J. Halley	cabinetmaker		
17	G. Coutts Douglas	lathsplitter	D. Chishom	stamp cutter
18	*As above*		P. Begg	warehouseman
19	R. Donald	reporter	G. Cropper	painter
20	*As above*		R. Stewart	druggist
21	R. Thomson	baker	J. Dickison	clerk
22	*As above*		Mrs Fyfe	

23	Miss Smith		D. Craill	bookseller
24	J. Nicol	painter		
25	D. Sinclair	clerk		
26	W. Beavis	brassfounder		
27	W. Davies	carver & gilder	Mrs Mathison	
28	J. Croall	joiner		
29	P. MacGregor		J. Ferrier	clerk
30	J. Pearson	joiner		
31	J. Hay	saddler		
32	J. Colville	mason		

Glenogle Place

Why so named?: By the time this row was built, the whole estate was named Glenogle Park (see page 53), so this was a logical choice of name.

Date when building began: 1868

Original selling price of the houses: No. 1 = £180, Nos. 2 and 3 = £150, No. 4 = £175, No. 5 = £200, Nos. 6 and 7 = £180, No. 8 = £210.

Notes, and features of interest: The design and finish of these houses is slightly different from any of the earlier ones, largely due to a request made by the potential buyers, who asked for them to be 'a little superior' owing to their less pleasant location, beside the main road (see page 31).

GLENOGLE PLACE: OWNERS/OCCUPIERS

No.	Owner	Occupation	Tenant	Occupation
1	S. Yarroll	furrier		
2	*As above*		S. Martin	hairdresser
3	J. Gilbert	waiter		
4	R. Neilson	baker	J. Risk	clerk
5	S. Yarroll	furrier	W. Stephen	shopman
6	G. Dickison	mason		
7	G. McDonald	waiter		
8	R. Neilson	baker		

Kemp Place

Why so named?: 'In compliment to Mr Kemp for the interest he had taken from the formation, in the Company's welfare.' These were the words recorded in the Cooperative's Minute Book on February 24, 1869. The Mr Kemp referred to was Daniel Kemp, Governor of the Edinburgh City Poor House on Forrest Road and one of the first shareholders in the Cooperative. His son, Daniel William, also joined the Company as a Director in about 1867. Since neither of them was a building operative, they could not hold the office of Company Chairman, though both of them served for some years as Vice-President and provided much of the financial guidance needed by the Cooperative in its early years.

Date when building began: 1868

Original selling price of the houses: £250 for upper river-end house (No. 16) and £200 for other upper houses without made-up attics. The rest not known.

Notes, and features of interest: Before building was completed, one of the Directors suggested that the last block at the river end should be made up of four smaller houses, with one front door for each pair. When plans were drawn, it was found to be impossible to fit four houses into the given area, so James Colville submitted a plan for two large houses instead. These two double-fronted houses became the first of their kind in the Colonies. Ironically, the earlier plan for four houses was later realised, at least in part, because in 1947, the upper house was divided into two separate dwellings. Many years before this division, in 1886, James Colville bought the house for £250 (the original selling price.) and he and his wife, two unmarried daughters and nineteen-year-old granddaughter moved in. This may account for the iron balconies and the elaborate ceiling mouldings in the house (see pages 31 and 32).

31 Upper (plasterer) and lower (joiner) plaques, Kemp Place.

32 This VE Day party was held in the street between Kemp Place (on the left) and Bell Place. The river-end house in Kemp Place is one of the few double-fronted houses in the Colonies, the upper part of which was once the home of James Colville and his family.

Kemp Place was the first to have carved gable-end plaques depicting the symbols of two of the trades represented amongst the Cooperative's share-holders and house owners, namely plasterer and joiner.

KEMP PLACE: OWNERS/OCCUPIERS

No.	Owner	Occupation	Tenant	Occupation
1	J. Hay	saddler	W. Cannon	printer
2	A. Jeffrey	plumber		
3	P. Binnie	railway servant		
4	T. Mason	joiner		
5	Mrs P. Keys		J. Buchanan	grocer
6	D. Lym	cabinetmaker		

7	Miss C. Haldane				
8	W. Begg	gardener			
9	A. Thomson	clerk			
10	H. Stewart	printer	J. Mather	gilder
11	Miss M. Smith		F. Watson	clerk
12	A. Craig	plumber		
13	J. Burns		Mrs Menzies	
14	W. Wright	clerk		
15	D. Grubb	clerk		
16	W. Aitken	collector		
17	J. Johnston	cook		
18	W. Paxton	joiner		
19	Mrs M. Rankin			
20	Miss M. Smith		W. McDougall	cashier
21	J. Coventry	cabinetmaker		
22	G. Miller	teacher		
23	J. Craig	compositor		
24	G. Purdie	turner		
25	A. Forsyth	gardener		
26	A Gibson	coachman		
27	W. Blyth	draper	J. Paul	baker
28	J. Blyth	mason		
29	W. Cook	hairdresser		
30	D. Peters	clerk		

Glenogle Terrace

Why so named?: To make a pair with Glenogle Place (see pages 53 and 57)

Date when building began: 1869

Original selling price of the houses: No. 1 = £145, Nos. 2-4 = £140, No. 5 = £155, Nos. 6-8 = £150.

Notes, and features of interest: This was the first terrace to be built with internal rather than external stairs giving access to the upper houses. The cost of building was therefore slightly higher, but the resulting loss of space made the houses rather less expensive than those in Glenogle Place. They did, however, have larger gardens and a much more congenial aspect.

GLENOGLE TERRACE: OWNERS/OCCUPIERS

No.	Owner	Occupation	Tenant	Occupation
1	H. Law	joiner		
2	Miss McRae		P. Robertson	clerk
3	*As above*		B. Robertson	
4	D. McRae	shopman		
5	T. Morrison	painter		
6	Mrs McNeill			
7	J. Lamb	carver		
8	J. Colville	mason	Mrs Jane Webster	
			D. Low	labourer

Avondale Place

Why so named?: No reason is given in the Company Minutes, but what is recorded is a proposal from one of the Directors to name it 'Weddell Place' as a compliment to George Weddell, one of the first Directors in the Company. For some reason, nobody seconded this proposal, so the fanciful choice of 'Avondale' was carried.

Date when building began: Late 1869

Notes, and features of interest: It was agreed that oriel (bay) windows should be added to every second pair of houses, and that the two river-end houses should be double-fronted. These (Nos. 15 and 16) were both bought by Alexander Calder, a monumental sculptor, who built a large, domed conservatory in the garden of No. 15 which stood there until the Second World War. Given the oriel windows, large gable-end houses, and the particularly elaborate ceiling cornices in many of the houses, Avondale Place was perhaps the grandest of all the Colonies terraces. Sadly, there is no record of the prices charged, but it seems likely that they were higher than those in either Kemp or Bell Places.

Numbers 1 and 30 were both bought by James Colville. His son, Andrew, followed by his daughter Isabella, lived at No. 30 for some years. Isabella was by then married to William MacDougall, a plumber, and they had two children, Elizabeth and Colville MacDougall.

AVONDALE PLACE: OWNERS/OCCUPIERS

No.	Owner	Occupation	Tenant	Occupation
1	J. Colville	mason	A. Shein	
2	G. Matheson	GPO stamper	D. Kennedy	joiner
3	T. Muir	cabinetmaker		
4	J. Simpson	pocketbook maker		
5	W. Kinnaird	confectioner		
6	T. Deas	french polisher		
7	D. Allan	clerk		
8	Miss J. Low		Mrs Paterson	
9	P. Hume	lighthouse inspector	(vacant)	
10	W. Millikin	cabinetmaker		
11	J. Cannon	clerk		
12	T. Peddie	civil engineer	H. Yates	compositor
13	A. Calder	sculptor	J. Bell	clerk
14	As above		J. Phillips	compositor
15	As above			
16	As above		D. Walker	traveller
17	As above		A. Kirk	clerk
18	As above		Miss Brown	
19	T. Rait	joiner	W. Bryson	gilder & carver
20	Miss I. Gray			
21	D. Rolls	accountant		
22	D. McNair	joiner		
23	Miss A. Dackers			
24	J. Burnett	butcher		
25	G. Paul	baker		
26	R. Leitch	baker		
27	J. Wilson	traveller	T. Horne	draper
28	A. Marshall	engraver		
29	G. Matheson	GPO stamper	J. Smeall	bootmaker
30	J. Colville	mason	A. Colville	compositor
			J. Forrest	bank clerk

33 Upper (plumber) and lower (blacksmith) plaques, Avondale Place.

Teviotdale Place

Why so named?: No reason is given in the Company records.

Dates when building began: 1872 for Nos. 1-8, 23-30; 1883 for Nos.-14, 17-22; 1908 for Nos. 15 and 16.

Notes, and features of interest: At the time when the first block was founded, the Cooperative's building yard and workshops occupied the northern end, next to the Water of Leith. This meant that only eight pairs of houses could be fitted into the space between Water Lane and the yard wall. By 1883, the wall had been demolished and there was room for a further six pairs of houses. Not until 1908, when the plasterers' shed had been removed, was the terrace completed. The last two houses (15 and 16) were the only ones in the terrace to be built with bathrooms.

34 Upper (trade not clear) and lower (decorator) plaques, Teviotdale Place.

TEVIOTDALE PLACE: OWNERS/OCCUPIERS

No.	Owner	Occupation	Tenant	Occupation
1	J. Colville	mason	Miss J. Bull	
2	W. Peddie		Mrs J. Drew	
3	T. Peddie	civil engineer	W. Forbes	gardener
4	*As above*		J. Thomson	draughtsman
5	T. Johnston	cooper		
6	R. McGowan	cooper		
7	G. Smith	baker		
8	J. Beveridge	shoemaker	R. Phillips	clerk
9	G. Paul	baker	A. Laurie	butler
10	G. Nicol	painter		
11	G. Milne	cabinetmaker		
12	W. Common	compositor		
13	J. Forrester	labourer	Mrs A. Forrester	bookbinder
14	R. Stewart	saddler		
15	H. Manchip	coppersmith		
16	C. Thomson	reader		
17	D. Ross	clerk		
18	J. Reid	joiner		
19	D. Chisholm	die cutter		
20	J. Croall	joiner	Mrs Gibson	lodging-house keeper
21	W. Munro	clerk		
22	A. Colville	watchmaker		
23	W. McAdam	bookbinder		
24	R. Brown	shoemaker		
25	A. Laurie	coachman		
26	T. Wood	bootmaker		
27	T. Peddie	civil engineer	D. McLaren	draper
28	*As above*		J. Johnstone	painter
29	W. Peddie		G. Johnstone	clerk
30	J. Colville	mason	M. Gunn	bookseller
			Harriet Notman	

Dunrobin Place

Why so named?: No reason is given in the Company Minutes. Dunrobin is the name of the castle which is the seat of the Dukes of Sutherland – a rather pretentious choice for a terrace of artisans' houses.

Dates when building began: 1872 for Nos. 1-4, 27-30; 1874 for Nos. 5-8, 23-26; 1908 for Nos. 9-15, 16-22.

Notes, and features of interest: As with Teviotdale Place, this terrace had to be built in stages due to the presence of the builders' yard at the northern end. The completion of the terrace in 1911 also marked the completion of Glenogle Park, hence the commemorative plaque on the last block of houses (No. 17). By that time, James Colville had been dead for nearly twenty years, and the Cooperative was under the management of George Mill, previously the foreman joiner of the Cooperative.

35 Upper (slater) and lower (carter) plaques, Dunrobin Place.

DUNROBIN PLACE: OWNERS/OCCUPIERS

No.	Owner	Occupation	Tenant	Occupation
1	W. McDougall	plumber	T. Dick	vandriver
2	D. R. Kemp		A. Mitchell	mason
3	G. Mill		W. Nurthen	compositor
4	J. Smeall	bootmaker	(vacant)	
5	J. Gibson	plasterer		
6	G. Reid		W. Torrance	feu collector
7	W. Crawford	joiner		
8	D. Brown	cabinetmaker		
9	P. Evans	water officer		

10	A. Caws	ship steward			
11	J. Leitch	compositor			
12	W. Birrell	mason			
13	Miss H. Wright	dairywoman	R. Wright		
14	H. Giles	police constable			
15	J. Bishop	litho machineman			
16	A. Miller	messenger			
17	J. Kelly	compositor			
18	P. Smart	tailor			
19	S. Milne	printer			
20	J. Reid	railway inspector			
21	Miss C. Crawford				
22	J. Johnston	joiner			
23	Rev. R Brown		ʲJ. McIntosh		
24	Mrs J. Smith		Mrs M. Stewart		
25	F. Brown	clerk	J. Crooke	shopman	
26	W. Ritchie	teacher			
27	T. Denholm	cartwright			
28	Mrs M. Black				
29	A Forsyth	gardener	J. Stewart		
30	J. Wilson	traveller	C. Boyd	traveller	

Balmoral Place

Why so named?: Presumably after Balmoral Castle.

Dates when building began: 1872 for Nos. 1-8, 23-30; 1873 for Nos.-12, 19-24; 1894 for Nos. 13-15, 16-18.

Notes, and features of interest: The completion of the last three pairs of houses was left until 1894 since the ground was occupied up until then by a laundry (previously Canonmills Cottages). These last houses were the first in the Colonies to be built with bathrooms and it may be an indication of the changing times and fashions that they were also all owner-occupied, unlike the earlier houses which were all let (see Table). There is in fact a record in the Company Minutes of James Colville asking for the Directors' approval for the sale of eight houses to one person (Thomas Peddie) – approval that was obviously given.

36 Upper (trade not clear) and lower (draughtsman) plaques, Balmoral Place.

BALMORAL PLACE: OWNERS/OCCUPIERS

No.	Owner	Occupation	Tenant	Occupation
1	T. Peddie	civil engineer	J. McIntosh	gardener
2	W. Peddie		J. McGie	compositor
3	T. Peddie	civil engineer	A. Robertson	carver & gilder
4	*As above*		W. Murtrie	hairdresser
5	J. Watt	shipmaster	J. Finlayson	butler
6	*As above*		A. Denholm	blacksmith
7	*As above*		T. Hay	mason
8	*As above*		Mrs Grace Thomson	
9	G. Reid	coachman	A. Robertson	wood turner
10	A. Cromb	writer	A. Smith	clerk
11	*As above*		A. McKenzie	baker
12	*As above*		T. Edgar	
13	J. Tocher	cabinetmaker		
14	A. Leitch	compositor		
15	J. McMinn	postman		
16	J. Auchinachie	janitor		
17	R. Neil	cabinetmaker		
18	T. Waite	joiner		
19	A. Cromb	writer	J. Neilson	grocer
20	*As above*		J. Lindsay	printer
21	*As above*		Mrs Blackie	
22	R. Harrower	tailor	G. Lawrie	greengrocer
23	J. Watt	shipmaster	J. Collie	coachman
24	*As above*		J. Symon	missionary
25	*As above*		Mrs S. Taylor	
26	R. Ketchen	butcher	A. Dunn	butler
27	T. Peddie	civil engineer	Mrs M. Cowan	
28	*As above*		J. Winnint	clerk
29	W. Peddie		W. Troup	compositor
30	T. Peddie	civil engineer		

Bridge Place

Why so named?: Because of its position next to the wooden footbridge which, at that time, was the main means of access to the Colonies from Stockbridge and Arboretum Road. Three years after Bridge Place was started, so was a new road bridge on the same site as the earlier footbridge. Built for £1000, this robust new bridge was paid for by the Town Council and City Road Trust, and opened in 1877 by the Lord Provost, James Falshaw. Not until 1956 was it resurfaced and rebuilt with concrete supports to carry the heavier loads of the mid-twentieth century.

Date when building began: 1872

Original selling price of the houses: Approximately £220 for a house, and either £300 or £350 for a shop.

Notes, and features of interest: This short row of houses and shops was built on the site of the Cooperative's first joiners' shed and office. Although the Company had built shops at several other sites in the city, these were the first to be specially built at Stockbridge, and for some reason proved to be quite difficult to sell. When two interested house buyers expressed concern at the Company's plan to build a bakehouse there, James Colville was so anxious not to lose the sales that he dropped the plan.

The use for the shops obviously changed several times over the years (see Figure 37. Not until the 1980s was the last of the shops finally converted into a house, making a complete terrace of houses out of what was originally a row of four houses and four shops.

BRIDGE PLACE: OWNERS/OCCUPIERS

No.	Owner	Occupation	Tenant	Occupation
1	Mrs Kelly		(vacant)	
2	Edinburgh Cooperative Building Co.		T. Hastie	baker
3	*As above*		G. Brown	grocer
4	*As above*		Miss Lyon	
5	*As above*		(vacant)	
6	W. Kirkpatrick	clerk		
7	W. Smith	carter		
8	J. McDougall	teacher		

37 The shops at Bridge Place, as they were in about 1902. It is not clear what all the shops were at that date, but at the time of the 1891 Census, they were – from left to right – No. 2 grocer, No. 3 unoccupied, No. 4 dairy, No. 5 grocer. Numbers 1, 6, 7 and 8 were houses without shops. In later years, the shops included a greengrocer, dressmaker and sweetshop.

Glenogle House

Why so named?: Presumably to be consistent with the two adjacent terraces – Glenogle Place and Terrace. Until the extension of the house in 1875, it had been known as Keif House, and appears on maps as Canonmills Cottage (see page 19).

Date when building began: The date of the original house, which now forms the core of Glenogle House, is probably around 1780; the same year that the Haig family built the neighbouring distillery. 1875 was the date of the conversion and extension by the Cooperative.

Original selling price of the houses: Following the extension in 1875, the new building comprised six separate dwellings, each of which was given a different price. One was priced at £280 (probably the centre house), three at £175 (perhaps 5, 7 and 8), and two at £180.

Notes, and features of interest: In the absence of any detailed plans of the original house, and of the plans for conversion, it is only possible to guess at the way in which the house was altered by the Cooperative in 1875. According to the Company Minutes, the first plan was actually to sell the house in its existing form, but this proved to be impossible under the terms of the feu charter. The next proposal was to demolish it altogether, presumably to make way for a completely new block similar to Glenogle Place or Terrace. Finally, however, the decision was taken to build on to the existing structure and to convert the resulting building into six separate dwellings. Wings were added at both sides of the centre house, and the rooms reapportioned so that the bulk of the ground floor could be turned into a separate flat (No. 7) with its own front door on the north side of the building.

According to the 1881 Census, as many as thirty-nine people lived in Glenogle House in that year, compared with nine a century later.

38 This picture of Glenogle House shows the original house in the centre, flanked by the two wings that were built by the Cooperative in 1875.

GLENOGLE HOUSE: OWNERS/OCCUPIERS

Owner	Occupation	Tenant	Occupation
James Colville	mason (Manager of ECBC)	Robert Davie	bootmaker
John Wilson	traveller		
James Deas	french polisher		
James Haggart	cabinetmaker		
Walter Beavis	brassfounder		
Frances Gray	Arnott painter		
(Individual house numbers not listed in original records)			

References

The following list names only those sources that were used extensively and/or which may be of special interest.

RECORDS

Census registers (1871, 1881, 1891)
Edinburgh Cooperative Building Company: Minute Books, Company ledgers, Articles of Association
Parish Valuation Rolls
Post Office Directories
Town Council Minutes
Personal papers of D. W. Kemp

PERIODICALS AND NEWSPAPERS

The Builder (November 2 and 30, 1861)
The Edinburgh Evening Courant (October 24, 1861; November 30, 1861)
Transactions of the National Association for the Promotion of Social Science (various papers for the years 1861-1863, 1866)

PUBLICATIONS

The Reverend Doctor James Begg, *Happy Homes for Working Men: and how to get them* (First Edition, 1866, Second Edition, 1872)
Elizabeth A. Filor, M.Sc. dissertation, *Victorian Working Class Housing in Edinburgh: A Comparison of the Different Types* (1973)
Sir Hugh Gilzean Reid, *Housing the People – An Example in Cooperation* (1894), *Social and Religious Life in the North*
Cumberland Hill, *Historical Memorials and Reminiscences of Stockbridge* (1877)
J. Laver, *The House of Haig*
Ian MacDougall (Ed.), *The Minutes of Edinburgh Trades Council, 1859-1873*
The Reverend Adam Mackay, *Distinguished Sons of Cruden*
W. H. Marwick, *Economic Developments in Victorian Scotland* (1936)
Dr. W. A. Munford, *James Duff Brown – Portrait of a Library Pioneer*
George Rosie, *Hugh Miller: Outrage and Order (1981)*
The Reverend Thomas Smith, *Memoirs of James Begg* (Vols I and II, 1888)